The Fourth of July

Debra Hess

BENCHMARK BOOKS

MARSHALL CAVENDISH

NEW YORK

SYMBOLS of AMERICA

Benchmark Books
Marshall Cavendish
99 White Plains Road
Tarrytown, NY 10591-9001
www.marshallcavendish.com

Library of Congress Cataloging-in-Publication Data

Hess, Debra
The Fourth of July / by Debra Hess.
   v. cm. — (Symbols of America)
Includes bibliographical references and index.
Contents: Taxation without representation—A nation is born—The American dream.
ISBN 0-7614-1711-7
  1. Fourth of July—Juvenile literature. 2. Fourth of July celebrations—Juvenile literature. [1. Fourth of July. 2. Holidays.]
  I. Title II. Series: Hess, Debra. Symbols of America.

E286.A1285 2003
394.2634—dc21

2003004934

Photo research by Anne Burns Images

Front and back covers: Corbis/Ariel Skelley

The photographs in this book are used by permission and through the courtesy of:
Corbis: Joseph Sohm, title page; Ariel Skelley, 4, 31; Bettmann, 8, 15; Bob Gomel, 27; Reuters NewMedia, 28; Strauss/Curtis, 32; Lester Lefkowitz, 35. Granger Collection: 7, 11, 12, 19, 20. North Wind Pictures: 16, 23, 24.

Series design by Adam Mietlowski

Printed in Italy

1 3 5 6 4 2

Contents

CHAPTER ONE
No Taxation Without Representation   5

CHAPTER TWO
A Nation Is Born   21

CHAPTER THREE
The American Dream   26

Glossary   36

Find Out More   38

Index   40

No Taxation Without Representation

Every year on July 4, in towns and cities across America, fireworks light up the sky. There are parades, parties, and picnics. Buildings are draped in red, white, and blue flags and banners. Ships sail into harbors with the *Stars and Stripes* rippling in the breeze. It is the day that Americans celebrate their *independence*. On July 4, 1776, the Declaration of Independence was approved, and America gained its freedom from England. But how did it all happen? And how did the Fourth of July become a national holiday?

◀ *Children like Fourth of July celebrations, especially when there are sparklers!*

The story begins in 1776. At that time, the United States of America did not yet exist. There were only thirteen *colonies* in what is now the eastern part of the United States. These colonies belonged to England. About 2.5 million people—called *colonists*—lived there. Each colony had a governor who reported to the British king.

Until 1776, the original thirteen colonies were still part of England. ▶

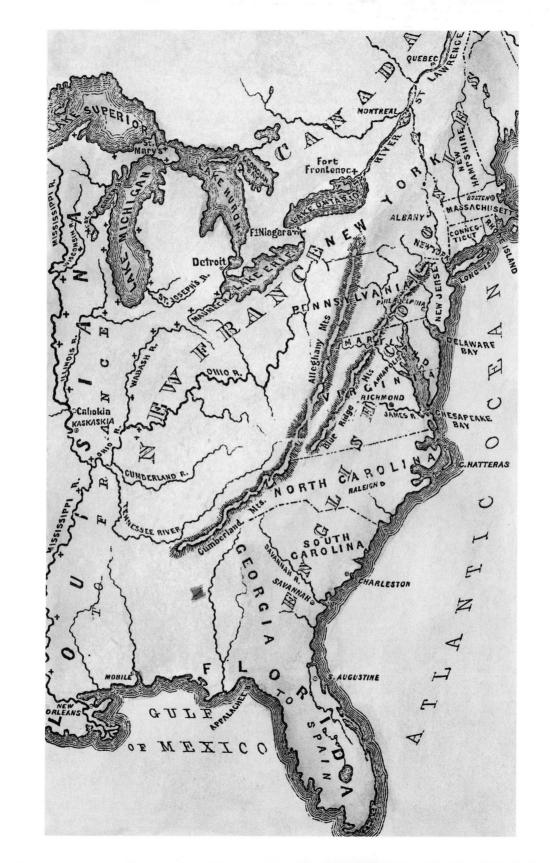

For many years the colonists were left to *govern* their part of the world in peace. But all that changed when a new English king came to the throne. In 1760 King George III was crowned. At the time, England was in the middle of a war with France that had begun in 1754 over control of North America. In America this war is known as the French and Indian War. In 1756 other nations in Europe joined France to fight England. The war, known in Europe as the Seven Years' War, was fought on land and sea until 1763.

In one important battle of the French and Indian War, the British took Quebec in Canada. French general Louis Joseph de Montcalm died during the fighting.

By the end of the war, England had spent so much money that the country was heavily in debt. King George III and the new British *prime minister*, George Grenville, made a decision that would change the face of the world. In 1763 they decided to make the colonists pay taxes to England. The first tax was on sugar.

At first, King George III did not realize how unpopular the taxes would be. ▶

Then, in 1765, the Stamp Act was passed. Colonists now had to buy tax stamps for all legal documents. Other paper products, such as newspapers and almanacs, needed a stamp as well.

The colonists were angry about the taxes. They had no *representation* in the British government and therefore no right to vote on any issue that affected them. Why then should they pay taxes to a country that gave them no rights?

◄ *The American colonists* protested *the Stamp Act by burning the British tax stamps in a bonfire.*

Across the colonies, people gathered to protest the taxes. They refused to shop in stores that sold products from England. At first the British government listened and ended some of the taxes. But new taxes on glass, paint, and tea soon followed. The colonists became even angrier.

Colonists pull over a statue of King George III to show their anger at his series of ▶ *new taxes.*

In 1773 a group of men boarded a British ship in Boston Harbor. The ship was carrying a cargo of tea for the colonies. The men dumped all the tea on board into the water. This event is known as the Boston Tea Party. The British responded by closing the port of Boston. The colonists were furious.

"No taxation without representation" became the cry of a young nation that decided to break free from England's rule.

Disguised as Indians, the American colonists dump tea into Boston Harbor.

King George III sent troops across the ocean. They were to control the angry colonists who had decided to unite. In 1774 all but one of the thirteen colonies sent *delegates* to Philadelphia, Pennsylvania (Georgia did not send delegates, but said it would support whatever decisions the other colonies made). The delegates formed the First Continental Congress. They agreed they all wanted changes. They discussed the best way to bring this about.

In May 1775 the colonists formed a Second Continental Congress. The congress spent almost a year trying to work out the problems with England. When that didn't work, the delegates declared war. The American Revolution had begun.

George Washington travels with two other delegates to the First Continental Congress at Philadelphia in 1774.

▶

CHAPTER TWO

A Nation Is Born

On June 7, 1776, a delegate named Richard Henry Lee asked the Second Continental Congress to declare the colonies free from England. The other delegates liked the idea and agreed that they needed a formal document. Although several people had ideas about what the document should say, it was Thomas Jefferson who actually wrote the Declaration of Independence.

Jefferson wrote a first draft and showed it to Congress on June 28, 1776. The final document was not approved until late on the afternoon of July 4.

◄ *In addition to being a strong leader, Thomas Jefferson was a talented writer as well.*

The next day, copies of the Declaration of Independence were passed out to the delegates and to various newspapers in the colonies. On July 6 the *Pennsylvania Evening Post* became the first newspaper to print the new document. On July 8 it was read out loud in Philadelphia's Independence Square while a bell rang and crowds cheered. The bell in Independence Square would later be known as the Liberty Bell.

Did You Know?

Another symbol of American freedom is a 2,000-pound (907-kg) bell called the Liberty Bell. The bell is now most famous for the crack that left it useless. But at the time of the signing of the Declaration of Independence, it was a working bell that hung in Philadelphia, Pennsylvania. On the Fourth of July in 1776, the leaders of all the American colonies were in Philadelphia. When they approved the Declaration of Independence, the bell rang out to bring the people of Philadelphia together to hear the news that they were now free.

The Declaration of Independence was read out loud by a man named John Nixon while a crowd outside Independence Hall in Philadelphia cheered.

The signing of the Declaration of Independence was not completed until August 4. But the first celebration took place a month earlier on July 4. From then on, the Fourth of July has been viewed as America's birthday. Since the early 1800s and to this day, Americans have been setting off fireworks, hosting parades, and attending picnics to celebrate America's freedom.

◀ *Over the years, the Fourth of July has been celebrated in many different ways. This event took place in Centre Square in Philadelphia in 1819.*

CHAPTER THREE

The American Dream

Although the Declaration of Independence was not completely signed until August, the Fourth of July has been celebrated as Independence Day since 1776. In the years that followed, large public celebrations with parades, speeches, and fireworks sprang up around the newly freed country. Sometimes cannons were fired into the air.

Today many cities celebrate the Fourth of July with fireworks displays, such as this ▶ *one over Houston, Texas.*

July 4 became a legal holiday in 1941 when Congress signed it into law. Today Americans still have picnics and fireworks on the Fourth of July, but cannons are no longer allowed. In Bristol, Rhode Island, fire engine companies host water-squirting contests; in Wisconsin, the holiday is celebrated as Indian Rights Day; and in Flagstaff, Arizona, Native Americans stage a three-day powwow with traditional tribal dances and rodeos.

◀ *Tugboats spray red and blue water in front of the Statue of Liberty: one of the many ways New Yorkers celebrate Independence Day.*

In Florida a 400-mile (644-kilometer) stock car race is held; in Lititz, Pennsylvania, a festival of candles lights up the sky; in Alaska the Inuit people compete in a whale-catching contest. Every Fourth of July Americans all across the United States celebrate the birth of their nation and their enduring independence.

Did You Know?

Uncle Sam is a character that leads many Fourth of July parades. He is usually dressed in striped pants, a tailcoat, and a top hat decorated with the Stars and Stripes.

What many people don't know is that Uncle Sam was a real person. His name was Samuel Wilson. He was born in 1766 in Arlington, Massachusetts. After fighting in the American Revolution, he moved to Troy, New York, where he worked as a meatpacker. During the War of 1812, he supplied meat to the U.S. Army. One day, a group of people visited Wilson's plant. When they noticed that all the barrels of meat were stamped with the letters US, they asked what they stood for. "Uncle Sam," said a worker. "Uncle Sam Wilson—the man who supplies meat to the army."

When this story was written up in a local newspaper, Uncle Sam became famous. In 1869 a well-known cartoonist drew a picture of Uncle Sam with a beard. He has been a symbol of America ever since.

Children wave their American flags during an Independence Day parade in Accomac, Virginia. How does your community celebrate?

Every Fourth of July Americans have the chance to show their pride in their country. In between the picnics and the fireworks, people across the United States ask themselves if we have created the nation our *forefathers* had in mind. Are we really a land of *opportunity* for all people? Do we treat our citizens equally? Are we living in a country our children will be proud of?

◀ *Two proud Americans: a mother and son embrace on the Fourth of July.*

As we celebrate Independence Day each year, it is important to remember how hard our forefathers fought for *liberty*. The Fourth of July marks the birth of a strong and unique nation. For more than 225 years, the ideas of freedom and liberty first set down in the Declaration of Independence have kept America united and strong.

The Fourth of July may be a great time to have fun with family and friends. It is also the perfect chance for all Americans to think about freedom, a gift we enjoy not only on the Fourth of July but every day of the year.

On the Fourth of July, colorful fireworks light up the night sky all across America. ▶

Glossary

colonist—A settler.

colony—A territory that has been settled by people from another country and is controlled by that country.

delegate—Someone who represents other people at a meeting.

forefather—An ancestor.

govern—To rule, control, or manage.

independence—The ability to stand or act alone; freedom.

liberty—Freedom.

opportunity—The chance to improve or better one's self.

patriotic—Showing love and loyalty to one's country.

prime minister—The leader of a nation's government.

protest—To challenge a rule or law thought to be unfair.

representation—Having someone speak or act for a group of people.

Stars and Stripes—A nickname for the American flag.

Find Out More

Books

Ansary, Mir Tamim. *Independence Day.* Crystal Lake, IL: Heinemann Library, 2001.

Graham-Barber, Lynda. *Doodle Dandy! The Complete Book of Independence Day Words.* New York: Simon & Schuster, 1992.

Landau, Elaine. *Independence Day: Birthday of the United States.* Berkeley Heights, NJ: Enslow Publishers, 2001.

Sanders, Nancy I. *Independence Day.* Danbury, CT: Children's Press, 2003.

Web Sites

American Independence Day: Fourth of July Theme
http://www.atozteacherstuff.com/themes/july4th.shtml

Fourth of July
http://www.kidsdomain.com/holiday/july4/

The Fourth of July Database
http://www.american.edu/heintze/fourth.htm#Designation

Fourth of July Links
http://www.yahooligans.com/Around_the_World/Countries/United_States/
Holidays/Fourth_of_July/

History of the Fourth
http://www.pbs.org/capitolfourth/history.html

Independence Day Crafts
http://www.kidsdomain.com/craft/_4th.html

Index

Page numbers in **boldface** are illustrations.

American Revolution, 18, 30

Boston, **16**, 17
Boston Tea Party, **16**, 17

cannons, 26, 29
celebrations, types of, 29–30
Cohan, George M., 17
colonies, 6, **7**, 14, 17, 18, 21, 22
colonists, 6, 9, 10, **12**, 13, 14, **15**, **16**, 17, 18
Congress,
    First Continental, 18
    Second Continental, 18, 21
    U.S., 29

Declaration of Independence, 5, 21, 22, 25, 26, 34
delegates, 18, **19**, 21

England, 5, 6, 10, 14, 17, 21

fireworks, **4**, 5, 25, 26, **27**, 29, 33, 34, **35**
flags, 5, 30, **31**, **33**
France, 9
French and Indian War, **8**, 9

George III, King, 9, 10, **11**, 14, **15**, 18
government, British, 13, 14
Grenville, George, 10

holiday, national, 5, 29

Independence Hall, 22, **23**

Jefferson, Thomas, **20**, 21
July 4, 5, 21, 25, 29

Liberty Bell, 22
Lee, Richard Henry, 21

Montcalm, Louis, **8**, 9

Native Americans, 29, 30
newspapers, 13, 22

Nixon, John, 22
North America, 9

parades, 5, 7, 25, 26, 30, **31**
Philadelphia, 18, 22, **23**, **24**, 25
picnics, 5, 25, 29, 33
protests, **12**, 13, 14, **15**

Seven Years' War, 9
Stamp Act, 13

tax, 10, 13, 14

Uncle Sam, 30

"Yankee Doodle Dandy," 17

Washington, George, 18, **19**
Wilson, Samuel, 30